STANDING
in the
COUNCIL
of the
L O R D

Carlton Kenney

Standing in the Council of the Lord
Copyright © 2002 by Carlton Kenney

Distributed by MorningStar Publications,
Division of MorningStar Fellowship Church
P.O. Box 19409, Charlotte, NC 28219-9409

International Standard Book Number 1-929371-11-X

MorningStar's website: www. morningstarministries.org
For information call 704-522-8111.

All Scripture references are New American Standard Version unless
otherwise indicated.

Cover Design & Book Layout by Dana Zondory

Table of Contents

INTRODUCTION

❦

In March of 1989 I attended a gathering of brethren who have a touch of the prophetic in their ministry. It was a small conference convened for the purpose of hearing what God was speaking concerning various issues. Though I make no personal claims to the prophetic office, I counted it a privilege to be around them. I not only attended the conference, but also conducted a Bible study each morning before they aired the weightier matters we had gathered to consider.

The subject I pursued in three sessions was entitled "Standing in the Council of the Lord," which I took from Jeremiah 23:18. In that passage the prophet deals with the problem of spurious visionaries who lay claim to his office. Those pretenders were challenged with various questions when God spoke through His servant. The following question is what I built this Bible study upon:

"But who has stood in the council of the Lord, that he should see and hear His word? Who has given heed to His word and listened?"

One subject that fascinated us was the claims made by various people regarding unusual audiences with God. We not only discussed visions, but out-of-body experiences as well. Some talked about personal conversations with God or with angels as though they were a commonplace experience. For any earnest believer the prospect of intimate communion with God is enticing, to say the least. However, our special area of interest revolved around the prophetic office. Having audiences with God is indispensable for those called to that ministry. Therefore, it was reasonable for us to ask, "What *does* it mean to stand in the council of God?"

If that question was timely then, it is even more so now. The controversy surrounding the prophetic ministry has not subsided in the last few years. Some have probably grown weary of the commotion, wishing it would go away. Yet, our instincts tell us that will not happen. The very fact that it will not *go away* testifies to the importance of the ministry. I suspect that the travail the church is going through now over this issue is most significant.

I did not attempt to discuss the prophetic role in general. My burden then and now in this publication concerns only one thing—*encounter with God*. I suppose this subject especially interests me because of an apprehension I have detected in discussions of the subject.

During the years of controversy, I have concluded that the main cause of alarm concerns the fear of people becoming too mystical. The opponents are not sounding the alarm concerning "prophets" possibly leading us astray, *but merely because the prophets are having these mystical experiences.* If visionaries are leading us down a road to moral compromise, or if they are crossing the boundaries of orthodoxy regarding the faith, we should be alarmed. However, the main point of contention is because some people are having mystical experiences.

An article in one leading evangelical publication quoted some criticisms that were leveled against perceived abuses of the prophetic. One of the charges in that article said these *prophets* "...promote unbiblical activities such as out-of-body experiences." Is the writer saying that out-of-body experiences are unbiblical? Is he saying that seeking such experiences is unbiblical? If the former, then I heartily disagree with that statement! If the latter, I would say it is not categorically wrong, but would depend upon a number of related factors.

In another case, a sincere pastor sought to warn his congregation about a "prophet" in the area. He developed his message around Paul's teaching in Colossians concerning inappropriate mysticism. He referred to this "prophet" as one who claims that angels speak to him. His next remark was that this is a horrible problem. If the brother meant that the problem existed because the ministry in suspect was leading people into immorality or propagating heresy, he was justified in his alarm. To warn people is what any faithful leader should do. However, in the context of his statement it sounded as if the problem was just the fact that the man was too mystical.

In the Orient, mysticism is a way of life. The churches in Eastern lands accept it as commonplace for saints to encounter heavenly messengers, or to be caught up into the presence of God when they pray. They do not regard it as the franchise of only a few who are called to Ephesians 4:11 ministry. Rather, it is the common privilege of a church in the midst of real war and deprivation. A church that desperately feels the need of help from on high does not fear becoming too mystical. This does not mean that readily accepting mystical experiences relieves the church of the necessity of proving all things. It does, however, reflect a difference in attitude between East and West.

I do not wish to say anything in this study to weaken the resolve of God's people to test the spirits. I identify with all believers who yearn for standards of excellence in conduct, and insist on orthodoxy in faith. My objective is to address an attitude in the Western church that affects us more than we are willing to acknowledge. We Westerners consider our pragmatism normal. We do not realize the extent it limits our acceptance of God-ordained, biblically defined mysticism. At best, we allow that these unusual experiences could occur *for some*. Yet, we have made up our minds concerning the frequency or regularity that it will happen. At worst, we reluctantly acknowledge that the Bible records such experiences, but wish to relegate it to a past era. We look askance at any who lay claim to these experiences today.

In this study I hope to lay bare Western prejudice, and to develop a biblical basis for meeting with God. My first priority is to show how vital this is for the prophetic office. I wish we would deny them nothing that pertains to their calling. I desire that they have the richest possible access to the presence of God. That is my first priority, but prophets are not the only group I consider. May God grant us *all* a greater understanding of the accessibility we have to the throne. May that understanding provoke us to renewed determination to avail ourselves to that access.

CHAPTER ONE

❧

THE MEANING OF COUNCIL

Our study will center on the provoking question posited by Jeremiah concerning standing in the counsel of God. The Hebrew word rendered in Jeremiah 23:18 as **"counsel"** or as **"council"** in other translations is *sode*. It does not occur many times in the Bible, but it has a precise and rich meaning. *Strong's Concordance* defines it primarily as "a session." It is a company of persons in close deliberation. Some occurrences of the word extend the meaning to "intimacy, consultation, or a secret." However, as we study the various occurrences of the word, we discover four aspects of its meaning.

One aspect of the meaning is "the people themselves who make up the group." In other words, it is *the council*. When Job lamented the loneliness he experienced in his trial he said, **"All my *associates* abhor me, and those I love have turned against me" (Job 19:19).** The New International Version renders **"associates"** as **"intimate**

friends" and *Young's* defines it as "the men of my counsel." Some proverbs extol the wisdom of having *counselors* around when plans are made (see Proverbs 15:22). When the patriarch Jacob was blessing two of his sons, he disassociates himself from their cruelty by saying, **"Let my soul not enter into their *council*; let not my glory be united with their assembly" (Genesis 49:6).** In this last reference the usage does not merely emphasize the persons, but also the fact of their coming together in wicked **"assembly"** to contrive their device.

Jacob's statement above alludes to the second aspect or nuance of *sode*. It is the act or process of the persons coming together and entering into deliberations. Speaking prophetically of the betrayal of Christ, the psalmist said, **"...it is you, a man my equal, my companion and my familiar friend. We who had sweet *fellowship* together, walked in the house of God in the throng" (Psalm 55:13-14).** In another psalm the righteous ones ask God to protect them from the devices of the wicked. **"They make shrewd *plans* against Thy people, and conspire together against Thy treasured ones" (Psalm 83:3).** Also, the psalmist cries, **"Hide me from the *secret counsel* of evildoers, from the tumult of those who do iniquity" (Psalm 64:2).** In this case it seems he hopes for a place of obscurity when those evil counselors come together.

A third aspect of the word *sode* concerns the information that is deliberated or the things that are purposed within that conclave. In the preceding paragraph we said that the psalmist is asking God to hide him from an evil assemblage. This could also convey another thought. Since his enemies knew about him, they came together for evil deliberations. His hope was that God would protect him from the plans devised against him. In this case the meaning refers not only to the coming together of the counselors, but the results of their deliberations. In other words, he cried to God so their plans would not succeed.

We see this idea also in the way Eliphaz challenges Job, **"Were you the first man to be born, or were you brought forth before the hills? Do you hear the *secret counsel* of God, and limit wisdom to yourself? What do you know that we do not know? What do you understand that we do not?" (Job 15:7-9).** The New International Version renders the question in verse 8: **"Do you listen in on God's council?"** That could mean that Eliphaz was asking Job if he was where the council was deliberated, but that was not likely in this case. When considered with the rest of the questions, it is more likely that Eliphaz was asking Job if he really was informed. Did he really hear those deliberations *and retain it as his source of knowledge?*

The final aspect of *sode* is intimated in the discussion of Eliphaz's question. **"Counsel"** also has the idea of the place where deliberations transpire. In that case, it would be "council," and not "counsel." **Psalm 111:1** as follows: **"Praise the LORD. I will extol the LORD with all my heart in *the council* of the upright and in the assembly"** (NIV). Such a statement is not concerned with what the counselors are doing, or the nature of their deliberations. Rather, the writer simply expressed the desire to be present in such a wonderful place. In that awesome setting he saw an opportunity to render praises to God.

In conclusion, the complexity should be obvious from the way I have analyzed the usage of the word to distinguish these four aspects. It is difficult in most cases to detect a single aspect in the usage of *sode.* These four shades of meaning often overlap. In most cases *more than one* of these ideas will fit the way the word is utilized. Nevertheless, I have tediously made those differentiations in order to isolate this fourth aspect—the idea of *place*. We are not surprised that the aspect of *place* is not emphasized when the mere councils of men are discussed. However, when we consider the council of God and *where* deliberations occur, it becomes more significant.

The psalmist said, **"The heavens will praise Thy wonders, O Lord; Thy faithfulness also in the assembly of the holy ones. For** who in the skies is comparable to the Lord? Who among the sons of the mighty is like the Lord, A God greatly feared in *the council* of the holy ones, and awesome above all those who are around Him?" (Psalm 89:5-7). The writer suggests that somewhere in the abode of God there is a conclave of "**holy ones**" who are identified as members of a council. We naturally expect that these members are creatures of an angelic order. That alone is enough to alert us that this place is in the heavenlies—a realm with which we are not naturally oriented.

Just the unnaturalness of this place is amazing enough. We must also consider the One who is central to the council. As much as any of the members of that council might impress us, they cannot compare with the Lord. The holiness, the majesty, the greatness of our God sets him apart in an indescribable way. That is the weight of meaning of those few words of the psalmist. We are speaking of our God "...**who is the blessed and only Sovereign, the King of kings and Lord of lords; who alone possesses immortality and dwells in unapproachable light; whom no man has seen or can see**" (I Timothy 6:15-16).

Considering the frailty of our humanity, to say nothing of our fallen nature, this certainly sets apart the place of His council. Many are skeptical of those who claim to have been *there*. Nonetheless, the implication of

Jeremiah's question is astounding. His question to the spurious visionaries suggests that there is some sense in which true messengers of God are granted audience in that place.

When Jeremiah challenged the credentials of his contemporaries, he might have worded it differently. He could have said, "Who has really heard God speaking to him, has perceived and heard His word?" Had the query been framed in those terms, it would be a language more familiar to us. We would anticipate the scene of sincere saints alone in their prayer closets, hearing God speaking into the depths of their hearts. That is so precious, and so basic to everything in the Christian life. In no way do I minimize that aspect of prayer. However, the language of the text suggests more than just a private communication between God and His devotee.

Sode at least refers to *members* of a council. Yet, certainly in the case of God's *sode* there is a *place*. Consequently, it is hard for us to limit the sphere to the confines of a prayer closet. The question is not, was God in the prayer closet, but was the praying saint there. That may seem like an unnecessary distinction, but as we go on in this study, I trust it will make sense. We must consider the prospect of the messenger of the Lord standing there. Thus, the logical place for us to begin our investigation is the throne room.

CHAPTER TWO

❦

THE THRONE ROOM

John, of all the Bible writers, had the most extensive revelation of the throne room. In Revelation 4, he gives a somewhat detailed description of the throne. He especially makes some remarks about God the Father, who majestically occupies that place. In Revelation 5, the narrative tells the posture of the Son of God in this whole scene. From apparently nowhere He is suddenly there in the midst of it all. The various groups around the throne incessantly adore Him. He is the One who has received the seven-sealed scrolls from the Father's hand. He is the Chief Facilitator. In Isaiah's words, He is the One in whose hand the will of Jehovah prospers (see Isaiah 53:10).

Isaiah also had access to this place; he gives a much briefer description than John, but the details are fascinating. He concentrates his description on only one group around the throne, the seraphim. From his description of these noble creatures, it appears that they are the four living creatures John saw. In both accounts these angelic beings are the closest group to the throne. In both descriptions their role is the same. They lead the other groups in worship. The only *real* difference in the two descriptions is their posture. John portrays them as stationary around the throne, whereas Isaiah portrays them in motion above the throne. Despite the similarities, some may feel that these are actually two different orders of angelic beings. For the sake of this study I will assume they are the same. In any case, this group closest to the throne is facing in that direction. They are wholly consumed with what they behold! Let us make some observations.

First, it is safe to assume that this is indeed a *place*, the abode of God. In Paul's writings he speaks much about a spiritual realm, which he identifies as the heavenlies. He says we are enthroned with Christ in that sphere, and He instructs us to conduct our struggle against wicked spirits in that sphere (see Ephesians 2:6, 6:12). It is the place where the church of Christ is to see herself in this present hour. Indeed, we determine life and death issues *to the extent we participate in that sphere*.

Since Paul describes this as normal Christian experience, we can conclude that our participation in the heavenlies is commonplace. To have access to that realm is the privilege of every believer. It depends only upon the redemption that procured us a position there, and our appropriating it by faith. However, technically speaking, Paul's heavenlies is not the place of which John and Isaiah speak.

Whereas the heavenlies are portrayed simply as another *realm*, heaven itself, the abode of God is described in terms of *location*. John's transition to that place came when a voice called him to *come up* there. God called him, and immediately he was in the Spirit *and there*. Paul, likewise, experienced that transition. When he relates how he experienced the divine Presence, he said he was *caught up* to that place. Moreover, he does not describe it as the normal experience of believers. In other words, this was something additional to our enthronement with Christ in the heavenlies. He speaks of it as a rare experience. To explain his ability to be there, he is forced to say something about his body. He must state whether he was in or out of his body. He identifies the place of this encounter as the third heaven in one verse and as Paradise in another (see II Corinthians 12:2-4). I assume Paul's third heaven is the same as John's and Isaiah's throne room.

Let us also notice the manner in which each of these men had their experience. We may refer to it as a vision, but in reality it was more than that. It was more than a revelation, an inner vision, or even a dream. In an unusual way these servants were permitted to actually be there. Paul, more than John or Isaiah, tediously explains the mode of his mystical experience. Isaiah, on the other hand, simply says that this was something he saw, which does not suggest something as sensational as Paul's out-of-body experience. Isaiah did not merely observe, but participated in what he was beholding. Otherwise, we might assume that he simply had a vision. Consequently, we realize that God granted these men an extraordinary audience. It was more than just an experience within their own being. Because of examples like this we must allow for the unusual. God does grant His people varying degrees of mystical experiences outside of their own being. In phenomenal ways they are permitted to stand in the council of God. Let us consider another throne room scene.

Ezekiel elaborately describes his vision of the throne in Ezekiel 1. Like John's vision in Revelation, his vision has the same three central features. There is the royal seat where the majestic One is enthroned. Second, there is the expanse or firmament, which forms the base for the throne. Last, there are four angelic beings attending to the throne. In this third point there are some fundamental differences, not only in their features, but also in their function. Whereas the four beings in Revelation have one face and six wings, the four living beings in Ezekiel all possess the same four different faces and only four wings. However, it is their function that impresses us the most.

We do not find the four in Ezekiel *on* the firmament positioned around the throne facing the center. Rather, they are circled *under* the firmament with their backs to each other. These intense creatures are facing each of the four directions. Moreover, there is the added feature of the curious wheels of exaggerated size seemingly in perpetual motion. Indeed, *motion* appears to be the striking feature of this composite throne picture.

Unlike the throne in heaven which is famous for being established, immovable, and the center of the universe, the throne from which God rules over all is continually moving. Furthermore, these four angelic attendants have the role of giving the throne mobility. Technically, this is not the exact same thing John saw when he was in the Spirit. So, what *is* this throne that Ezekiel saw? What is more important, where is this throne?

John describes the Lord Jesus as having **"seven eyes, which are the seven Spirits of God *sent forth into all the earth*"** **(Revelation 5:6 KJV).** I think those words contain what Ezekiel was privileged to behold. He watched the other end of that extension from the throne in heaven. As we contemplate this wonder, let us not forget God's purpose for this extra throne.

He does not send forth the Spirit into the earth just to bless humanity in an unconditional, vague way. The eyes of the Lord are not moving to and fro throughout the earth just looking for someone to bless, or someone who might receive a surge of divine power (see II Chronicles 16:9). The Father's purpose for the mediation of His Son *is to extend His throne into the earth*. According to the words of the Lord's Prayer, God ordains that His kingdom would come and His will be done on earth as it is in heaven.

Consequently, we do not locate Ezekiel's throne in the third heaven, but in proximity with man's abode. The eyes of the Lord are ranging here and there *throughout the earth*. We must not strain at the meaning of words, trying to force our present subject into a three-dimensional setting. On the other hand, neither can we make it totally ethereal and unrelated to our three-dimensional, time-space domain. In ways that almost defy words, the heavenlies are pressing in upon us. The kingdom of heaven is *at hand*—closer than we dare to believe! Even so, that closeness does not necessarily make it more accessible than the place Paul experienced in Paradise. Stated another way, *distance* is not what determines our being there.

Ezekiel was transported into the ecstatic state of visions a number of times. Among his many experiences there is no record that he ever entered the third heaven. Nevertheless, his many other experiences impress us. The record of one of these unusual visitations contains a very detailed description of a restored temple. Time loses its significance in this ecstatic state. God permits the prophet to go forward or backward in time, beholding things that have been or that will be. Nevertheless, I must stress these are more than inner experiences that affect him subjectively. In a real sense God's servant is there, and in some cases personally interacting with the event. His experience in the valley of dry bones is fascinating.

The common phrase Ezekiel uses to describe his transition into this ecstatic state is to say that the hand of the Lord came upon him. Seven times he mentions this. In six cases he describes his transition in such a way that we realize he speaks of out-of-body experiences (see Ezekiel 3:14; 8:3; 11:1,24; 37:1; 40:2). I cannot emphatically say that his encounter in Ezekiel 1 with the chariot-throne was an out-of-body experience, but assuredly it was more than a spiritual impression or inner revelation. In a life-changing way he experienced Him who reigns from the throne. God subsequently commissioned him for his task.

To complete our description of the place of God's council, let us look at one more throne scene taken from Daniel's experience.

> **"I kept looking until thrones were set up, and the Ancient of Days took His seat; His vesture was like white snow, and the hair of His head like pure wool. His throne was ablaze with flames, its wheels were a burning fire.**
>
> **A river of fire was flowing and coming out from before Him; thousands upon thousands were attending Him, and myriads upon myriads were standing before Him; The court sat, and the books were opened"** (Daniel 7:9,10).

We might suppose that this is a varied description of the throne room vision of Revelation, but the details reveal a difference. In this vision the throne of the Almighty is not firmly based upon the expanse John saw, but is in motion with its burning wheels. Also, the description of how this setting comes about speaks of something for the moment. The verb for placing the seats literally means they were thrown into position. Moreover, **"the Ancient of Days took His seat"** after this court was arranged—quite different from the throne of heaven that is *never* vacated. In heaven He is eternally "He who sits upon the throne."

The thrones in Ezekiel and Daniel's visions are similar inasmuch as they are both mobile. Daniel's throne, however, is more elaborate in its composition. Besides the presence of "the Ancient of Days" who has taken His seat, there is a group of honored personages who sit with Him in His council. I assume they are "the holy ones, the sons of the mighty" of whom the psalmist spoke. Moreover, around this group are innumerable angels, standing in readiness to execute the judgment of this council. What an awesome setting!

On the other hand, the throne Ezekiel saw is no less awesome, though simpler in its arrangement. The noise of many waters produced by the motion of the four cherubim implies myriads of angels nearby, attending the actions of this throne. In Daniel's vision there is only one throne or seat. Nothing is being deliberated. Heaven has decided! I conclude that this throne is an extension of what heaven's throne has deliberated.

What is the significance of the chariot-throne of Daniel? It certainly is a scene separate from the throne room of the third heaven. Somewhere intermediate to the third heaven and our domain, God is intervening in a decisive way at a crisis time in history. The setting for this event concerns the rise of the various world empires that resist the reign of God, asserting themselves over the nations. In particular this court is set at the time of the final empire when a notable rebel rises in power to be the antichrist. Are we to understand that this is a one-time event at the end of the age when the Most High will intervene in the heavenlies? Are we to interpret this as a general picture of how God will intervene at any crisis time in history? In any case, here we have another description of the council of God—similar, but different from the conclave in heaven.

In summary, the clearest idea concerning the relationship of visionaries to the council of God refers to them having audience before the throne in heaven, which is the *place* where God deliberates—His headquarters. Yet, we also see that intermediate to heaven and man's domain there is a spiritual realm— the heavenlies. In various ways God manifests Himself in this sphere, reveals His Word, and shows His plan to His servants. Whether in heaven itself, or in the heavenlies, there are various ways and varying degrees that we may enter the ecstatic state and be there. It now remains for us to consider what those ways are.

CHAPTER THREE

❦

BEING THERE

When Paul described his transition into the third heaven, he tried to explain how his physical being related to the process. He first said, **"...whether in the body I do not know, or *out of* the body I do not know."** He said in the next verse, **"...whether in the body or *apart from* the body I do not know..." (II Corinthians 12:2-3).** Maybe Paul did not intend a distinction between being out of his body or being apart from his body. Perhaps by these seemingly redundant statements he only meant to emphasize how unusual the experience was. At any rate, allowing that there *might* be a distinction, we will use that as a frame of reference for discussing communion in God's council. Hence, our study will follow by discussing experiences "*in* the body, *apart* from the body, and *out* of the body."

Experiences *in the body* are the kind that are most familiar to us. This is our normal walk with God. When we direct our thoughts heavenward, we anticipate God responding to us within our own being. Thoughts or feelings subjectively impress us in a manner that we learn to recognize as the voice of God. Besides this, there are the more vivid experiences such as dreams and visions. Joel's prophecy promises that the outpouring of the Spirit would include these visitations. Dreams, of course, occur in our sleep—they are not something we directly control. Visions occur in our waking moments. For some these can be clear mental pictures that occur while waiting upon God. In other cases the vision can occur outside of one's self, appearing before their eyes as a picture flashed on a screen.

Often there is no message given in these visions, leaving us with the challenge of interpreting them. Yet, sometimes God speaks to us audibly. At least two times God visited Paul during the night season, giving messages in visions (see Acts 16:9; 18:9). In those cases, the saint not only hears, but can also have dialogue with the messenger. When the Lord wanted to communicate with Ananias, He came to him in a vision and Ananias responded (see Acts 9:10). Also, when God sent an angel to speak to the Centurion, he came to him in a vision. He felt the angel was there in the room, and he fearfully conversed with him (see Acts 10:3-6).

What about experiences *apart from the body?* It is difficult to distinguish between these and some in the body experiences like we just discussed. We began our description with what is least extraordinary and ended it with open-eyed visions. Now we come to a category where the experiences are less subjective and more outside of ourselves. In other words, there is some question as to whether we experience it with our bodies or separately.

Trances fit into this category. Consider the difference between a vision and a trance. Perhaps we can say that with visions the people and events come to us, but in trances we go there. When Peter had his experience at Joppa it says **"he *fell into* a trance" (Acts 10:10).** Young's Literal Translation says, **"there fell upon him a trance."** Likewise, this happened to Paul in the temple. It literally says that he "came into a trance."

We might think it strange that those having these experiences could be so indefinite about what happens. They do not seem to know the difference between fantasy and reality. In the area between having a vision that they behold before their eyes (in some cases with dialogue) and having an experience where they momentarily fall into a subliminal state—at what point do they lose contact with their body?

Recall the account of Peter's deliverance from prison (see Acts 12:9-11). The angel awoke Peter, guided him past the first and second guard, out through an iron gate, and then disappeared. It was *after* all this before Peter realized it was not a vision. How could he walk so far, smelling the stench of the prison and all the other sensations to his senses, and still not know the reality of the situation? Is the line between subliminal experiences and reality that thin? Apparently so.

What can we say about experiences *out of the body?* I think it is even more difficult to distinguish between subliminal experiences apart from the body and experiences out of the body—*if indeed there really is a distinction.* I think the clearest case of being out of the body would be for one to have a trip to the third heaven. Paul's terminology for his trip is that he was caught up to that place. Yet, as unusual as that was, he still was not sure about his body.

There are numerous accounts of people in our day that lingered between life and death. For a while they experience a transition between this domain and the next. It seems they can look back and see their body and all the circumstances accompanying their apparent death. Without a doubt, death itself *is* the ultimate out-of-body experience. There is no question in the mind of the participant concerning what is happening. Notwithstanding, the Bible records examples of mystics who had similar experiences. Ezekiel's experience is a good illustration.

His second experience of the chariot-throne began one day when he was sitting in his house in Chaldea while in session with some of the elders of Judah. First, he said that the hand of the Lord fell upon him. Next, he looked and saw the glory that emanated from the throne—the same one he tells us about in Ezekiel 1. A hand proceeded from it, taking him by a lock of hair. He was lifted up between heaven and earth, taken in the visions of God to Jerusalem (see Ezekiel 8:1-3). This visitation continues for a few more chapters, finally concluding with this explanation: **"Afterwards the spirit took me up, and brought me in a vision by the Spirit of God into Chaldea, to them of the captivity.** *So the vision I had seen went up from me*" (Ezekiel 11:24 KJV).

What was this **"spirit"** that took him up in a vision by the Spirit of God? Was it his own personal spirit? Was it an angel? What was happening back in his house in Chaldea during this interim? Did he converse with the elders, or did they quietly wait for him to return from his trip? Ezekiel was quite a mystic! He felt no necessity as Paul to make distinctions of being in or out of his body. The spiritual realm and spiritual migrations were commonplace to him!

His trip into this segment of retroactive history has complex features to it. He not only saw and heard things, but also had

31

dialogue with the messenger. This only begins to describe the phenomenon. While on that trip he prophesied, and then actually saw the fulfillment of the prophecy. One of the immediate results of prophesying was for a man to die under the judgment of God! (see Ezekiel 11:13). What is it like for someone by the spirit to be lifted up and taken into the visions of God by the Spirit of God? Then, (while in that ecstatic state and on that trip) the Spirit of God falls upon them, causing them to prophesy? Were they not anointed from the beginning just to enable them to be on that trip? Is there such a thing as an anointing upon the anointing? I confess that such language goes far beyond my perception, but perhaps that reveals my Western mind-block.

Admittedly, I do not comprehend what it is to be anointed at some point while in a trance or on a trip. Nevertheless, such experiences were not as rare as we may want to believe. While on these trips those servants of God not only saw and observed, but also interacted with the scene before them. This occurred in such a way as to even *affect the outcome of the events.*

Ezekiel's experience in the valley of dry bones is a notable example. That event is still future, removed by hundreds of years from the time he participated in it. Nevertheless, the prophesying he did on that trip is just as powerful as if he were living in that future day when it will happen. What he did then is just as effective were he to be on the scene in the future to give those same prophesies again. God's Word will not return to Him void!

Also, Zechariah's experience is less familiar, but just as dramatic (see Zechariah 3:1-5). He was there! Up to a certain point he merely watched the struggle between the accuser and the angel of the Lord. He watched, listening in on the conversation concerning the high priest's position. Finally, he began to speak. He interceded *and the angels carried out his instructions.* Awesome!

In conclusion of this chapter, I laid out various ways that God's servants can be attuned to receive His Word. I began with the less sensational experiences—the commonplace communion that is most familiar to us. I proceeded toward the more unusual spiritual trips of mystics in the Bible. We did this by conveniently using the three terms: in the body, apart from the body, and out of the body. I particularly elaborated on experiences at the more phenomenal end of the spectrum, since this is where we are least acquainted (and tend to be skeptical). With this background, let us to look closely at these means of communing in God's council.

CHAPTER FOUR

⟨⟩

THE SIGNIFICANCE OF BEING THERE

Paul hesitated to talk about his experience, but had good reason to do so. Superfluous apostles had flaunted their credentials and swayed the Corinthians. Because of this, the Corinthians esteemed Paul less. They questioned his commission, this need in the church provoked Paul to boast of his credentials. Among the evidence he arrayed, he brought up visions and revelations of the Lord. He found in this a reason to glory. However, Paul is not glorying in the revelations themselves. He gloried in **"such a *one*" (II Corinthians 12:5 NKJV).** Stated another way, he recognized that it is an honor for God to entrust him with that experience (see II Corinthians 12:1-5).

I think this somewhat parallels the situation when Aaron and Miriam despised their younger brother and God intervened:

> **"...If there be a prophet among you, I the LORD will make myself**

known unto him in a vision, and will speak unto him in a dream.

My servant Moses is not so, who is faithful in all mine house.

With him will I speak mouth to mouth, even apparently, and not in dark speeches; and the similitude of the LORD shall he behold: wherefore then were ye not afraid to speak against my servant Moses?" (Numbers 12:6-8 KJV).

These words imply that God grants intimate audience with His servants in order to honor them. This idea is certainly at the heart of Paul's defense of himself (see II Corinthians 11:16-18, 30). God *had* honored him. Consequently, we must list this as one reason for God granting these exceptional experiences.

There is something else about these events that is more pertinent to this study. What is the significance of God using these ways for communicating with us? We readily recognize that part of the problem of standing in God's council concerns having a clear channel of communication. Granted that God truly is the One speaking, there are two things that distort, dilute, or otherwise complicate the message. The first is that we have to contend with the voice of enemy spirits. Second, God's Word must filter through our own thoughts and feelings.

Regarding the latter, if the means of communication is less subjective, then we are more removed from the process. If it is something that happens *to* us and not just *within* us, we can be clearer with regard to the source. Thus, we need to discern to what extent enemy sources have infiltrated the operation.

This is the essence of Peter's argument to his skeptical Jewish brethren in Jerusalem after his experience in Joppa (see Acts 11:5-18). He carefully explains that this was something that happened *to him* (something beyond his ability to manipulate). The revelation was contrary to his beliefs and his personal desires. In other words, it was not a subjective experience, but something beyond himself. So if he has stated his case truthfully, then people realize it is primarily a matter of discerning the other two possibilities. Was it God, or was it an enemy spirit? Hence, the more objective the means of communication, the easier it should be to discern the source.

Having said the above, I do not want to oversimplify the necessity of proving all things. Even if people have a relatively objective experience, it does not guarantee that the source will be purely one or the other. The church in these coming days is going to meet with higher levels of deception. When the occult and other phenomena in the enemy's camp are rampant, we cannot afford to be naive. However, for God to grant us a more objective means of standing in His council will facilitate the process. Let us now consider the factors relating to this communication.

When we have subjective experiences, we have the task of sorting through the revelation. We must determine whether our own thoughts influence us, or whether the enemy has infiltrated. When it is our own thoughts, there is no way we can see this. If we could see into the spirit realm, we could see the sources of the messages. When Zechariah had his experience (though he did not record what was said), he not only heard it, but also saw the adversary who was speaking.

Paul tells us so little about his trip to heaven. Did the angels of God escort him? On his way up did they meet with interference from principalities and powers in high places? We can only speculate, but I suspect that it was not difficult for Paul to discern between his enemies and his friends! I know of no other account in the Bible of a person who speaks so objectively about himself. He refers to himself as another man. That's really getting objective! Consequently, we can see how objectivity enhances the process of receiving the Word of God.

Having made so much of Paul's experience, I need to qualify one thing. Apparently God did not grant him that trip to heaven as a *means* of communicating a message. On the contrary, the Lord did not permit him to give us the message he received on that trip. Furthermore, we notice something else very important about this mystical process. He did not tell his experience in order to give credibility to his message. On another occasion when certain ones questioned his authority to receive divine revelation that would be canonized, he does mention the fact that he got it directly from God (see Galatians 1:11-17). In other words, the *means* by which God gave it to him was not the issue (dreams? an inner voice? open visions?). The message has been historically tried and confirmed. Paul's central message stands on its own merits. If someone comes later with a more superior means of revelation, it cannot abrogate the gospel (see Galatians 1:8-9). Therefore, we must be careful not to make the *means* of communication itself a criterion of what is true and what is not. Nevertheless, the means of communication *does* affect the way messengers stand in the council of the Lord and hear His Word.

I want to close this section by looking at an unusual promise in the Zechariah 3:7 given to Joshua the high priest.

"...If you will walk in My ways, and if you will perform My service, then you will also govern My house and also have charge of My courts, and *I will grant you free access among these who are standing here."*

The New International Version renders the promise as **"a place among these standing here."** The Revised Standard Version renders it as **"the right of access among those who are standing here."** Young's has it, **"I have given to thee conductors among these standing by."** So let us ask: Where is this place of which the promise speaks?

The key for understanding the promise is to establish precisely who was the group that was standing there. A group of *men* were present when Joshua received the promise. Immediately after giving the promise, the prophet makes much of the significance of Joshua and his assembled friends, declaring that they are a symbol. They are a prophetic sign of something God is going to do in the nation. The promise assigns a definite importance to the group of men assembled, but are they the group to which Zechariah refers?

It is difficult from the narrative to establish clearly who these men are. Were they elders of Israel? Were they another delegation of men returned from Babylon? (see Zechariah 6:10-15). Were they a group of priests? If they were any of these, what would be the significance of such a promise? The station and privilege of priests or elders could not compare with the office of the high priest. Before God, Joshua already possessed in his office, the highest privilege in the nation! Moreover, the prophet is speaking of a group *standing* by, whereas Joshua's friends are *seated* before him.

In Zechariah 4:1-3 the prophet has another unusual vision in which he sees the two olive trees with their curious arrangement **"one of the right side of the bowl and the other on its left side."** After pressing the heavenly messenger for an explanation, he finally tells the prophet, **"...these are the two anointed ones, who are standing by the Lord of the whole earth" (Zechariah 4:14).** Are these two men or two angels? It is not foreign in Scripture to speak of anointed angels, but it is peculiar to portray their anointing as something that is conducted to the people of God.

This picture was given to console Zerubbabel and his colleagues in their task of rebuilding. By this revelation they were to understand how they were succored from the heavenlies. In prison, Paul reaches out for help and expresses confidence that he will receive it through the prayers of the saints **"...and the supply of the Spirit of Jesus Christ" (Philippians 1:19 KJV).** These two olive trees are described in the richest possible terms. They are literally sons of fresh oil. It is staggering enough to contemplate the richness of what they receive, but that is not the extent of it. *The anointing does not stop with them.* Through the conduits there is a flow to the godly remnant that had returned from Babylon to rebuild.

Commentators seem to strain for an explanation of whom or what these two are.

One explanation says that they were not really personages, but symbolic of the agency through which the nation is helped— the regal office and the priestly office. It is strange to refer to the two offices as sons. Besides, there is the added difficulty of correlating this with the picture of the two witnesses in Revelation 11.

Had John simply mentioned two witnesses in a generic sense, we might treat them separately from Zechariah's vision. However, he dubs them as **"*the* two olive trees and *the* two lampstands that stand before the Lord of the earth" (Revelation 11:4).** He leaves no room to doubt that they are one and the same. When we consider the events surrounding these two in Revelation, that they are preachers, killed, raised from the dead, and ascend to heaven—it is difficult to imagine them as two offices or even as two angels. Consequently, allowing that these two are indeed *men* mightily anointed of God, we can only speculate as to who they are, and where this place is they stand. In any case, granted the ease in which Zechariah moves back and forth from the natural domain to the spiritual, it is not inconceivable that this "place" is somewhere in the heavenlies!

Supposing that the two witnesses are not the particular group the prophet referred to, let us look at the immediate setting in which he stated the promise. As we said above, there were no *men* standing by (other than Zechariah himself). Satan was standing on one side of Joshua and the angel of the Lord was in front, and there were unidentified attending angels standing around him (see Zechariah 3:4). Verse five speaks of still another when it says, "**...while the angel of the LORD was standing by.**"

I must conclude that this promised place of blessing is outside our domain, in the heavenlies where angels abide. Regardless of how strange this may seem to us, the promise invites Joshua to move freely in this realm. The prophets were already availing themselves of that promise. They apparently considered it a privilege inherent to their office.

Are we to relegate this promise only to the high priest office of the Old Testament? Does New Testament priesthood have less privilege? What about prophets today? I grant that there is a technical difference between the office of the Old Testament prophet and prophets today. Nonetheless, could it be we have relegated too much to the Old Testament era? Does our skepticism and pragmatism make it difficult for prophets today to move freely in the privileges of their office? May God grant us the humility of mind to be objective and unbiased! May He help us to freely receive any promise extended to us *in general*, and to His prophets *in particular*!

CHAPTER FIVE

❧

FACTORS PERTAINING TO BEING THERE

Thus far we have depicted the counselors of God's *sode* as angels. I do not rule out the possibility that redeemed creatures in heaven (e.g. the twenty-four elders) are also part of the council. I now want to introduce the idea that prophets, who are granted audience in that place, are also these intimate friends. This means there is a frightening sense in which God confides in them and deliberates with them. Amos says, **"Surely the Lord GOD does nothing unless He reveals His *secret counsel* (*sode*) to His servants the prophets" (Amos 3:7).** This promise does not obligate God to bring *all* His prophets into that confidence, but it does intimate that He plans to always have *some* of them around when He deliberates.

I am not saying that those in the prophetic office are the only ones privileged to have this unusual access. The New Testament abounds with promises to all saints to draw near with a true heart in full assurance of faith. The Lord is rich unto *all* that call upon Him. For many humble seeking brothers or sisters, that richness surely includes experiences of being there. Hence, though I am not excluding anyone merely because they are not in the prophetic office, I am making a case for the privilege of the office. It especially pertains to the prophets who stand in the council of God. However, is the privilege of the office, or the dynamic of the gift alone enough? By privilege of those two things, can one alone enter into that blessed communion?

"For the crooked man is an abomination to the Lord, but He is intimate (*sode*) with the upright" (Proverbs 3:32). The New International Version states: (He) **"takes the upright into His confidence."** When the ascended Christ gives gifts to men, two things are not inherent in that giving— moral character and proper order. The *character* must be formed and the *order* must be learned. The scary thing is that the gifts will work to a degree and for a season with deficiencies in either of those two things. That means there is a grace under which vessels, just because of their prophetic gift, will experience certain ease in being attuned. This is something other saints may not realize. By ease, I do not mean that they are lazy, or that they do not seek the Lord. It simply means that they are perceptive to the spiritual realm more than others. How will

46

they be true friends of God if there are glaring flaws in their character? The breach of morality is the issue in Jeremiah 23. Consider some of their sins.

He says that both prophet and priest are polluted; pollution has gone forth into all the land (see Jeremiah 23:11,15). The word "pollution" could cover a wide range of meaning, but Jeremiah 23:13 alludes to a special evil: **"They prophesied by Baal and led My people Israel astray."** These prophets are standing in the wrong council! They are getting it from the wrong source. For those who never knew the Lord and pass themselves off on the people as prophet, we can rightly call them false. They have no recourse but to give themselves to the wrong source of revelation. What about those who at one time were true prophets and later make concessions in moral conduct? Can their God-given gifts be perverted; can they mix the source of their knowing? Those are tough questions! Ezekiel says they see vanity and lying divination (see Ezekiel 13:6 KJV).

Another sin Jeremiah faults these messengers with is adultery (see Jeremiah 23:14). In a day when the sanctity of marriage is under attack, we cannot say too much to uphold the seventh commandment. The Lord has not changed His mind about excellent standards for marriage. Those who are the Lord's envoys must live up to those noble standards. They must model what it means for two people to be faithful in marriage.

In the same verse Jeremiah mentions the importance of sincerity. He says that the prophets walk in falsehood. The New International Version rendering is most vivid by saying they live a lie. Jeremiah 23:16 describes one way this occurs. **"They speak visions from their own minds, not from the mouth of the LORD (NIV)."** Not all would-be prophets fall so grievously as to give themselves over to occult forces. Nevertheless, if they do not esteem sincerity and absolute honesty, their own hearts will deceive them.

Again in **Jeremiah 23:30** he faults them for their deceitful ways. He says they **"steal My words from each other."** We might call this prophetic plagiarism. It is certainly lying when people speak words that are not the truth. These prophets were speaking God's Word, but *not a Word that God had spoken to them!*

Solomon says that pride goes before destruction and a haughty spirit before a fall. Pride and vanity in ministry will bring any of us down from the place of favor with God. He says that **"their course also is evil, and their might is not right" (Jeremiah 23:10).** The New International Version has it they **"use their power unjustly."** Gifted vessels that do not have moral restraints firmly built into them are dangerous to the ministry!

Power does corrupt in those cases. Finally, in Jeremiah 23:32 he faults them for **"reckless boasting."**

It is sad when leaders relax moral restraint and fall. We hope they will eventually feel remorse for their actions, regretting the bad influence it has upon God's people. If they will remove themselves from the place of leadership and submit themselves to restoration, the damage can be minimized. We feel compassion for them. However, when visionaries are defiant in their erring—changing the message and intentionally leading the people astray—those cases are so grievous. In Jeremiah 23:14 he rebukes such revolt saying, **"...they strengthen the hands of evildoers."** Jeremiah 23:17 states **"they keep saying to those who despise Me, The Lord has said, 'you will have peace.'"** Ezekiel records a similar complaint.

We could mention other things to describe God's friends—those whom He desires to bring into His confidence. We will let James sum it up for us:

> **"You adulteresses, do you not know that friendship with the world is hostility toward God? Therefore whoever wishes to be a friend of the world makes himself an enemy of God"** (James 4:4).

Those are strong words, but we need to hear them. Indeed, if we hope for real intimacy, we must heed those words. If we expect God to really bring us into His confidence, we must share His values. We must feel the way He feels about things.

Of all that we have previously said, there is yet one more thing that puts a seal on the matter:

> **"Who is the man who fears the LORD? He will instruct him in the way he should choose...**
>
> **The *secret of the LORD* (*sode*) is for those who fear Him, and He will make them know His covenant"** **(Psalm 25:12,14).**

For *sode* in Psalm 25:14 (NIV) it says, **"the Lord *confides* in those who fear Him."** The Bible has so much to say about the fear of the Lord! Yet, there seems to be such a deficiency of this in the church today. We must recognize its importance. It is the beginning place, the foundation of everything else in the kingdom of God. It is the commodity that puts everything into perspective, releasing God's blessings to us. It is a fountain of life (see Proverbs 14:27). It is the key that unlocks the treasures of God! (see Isaiah 33:6 NIV).

Perhaps one reason for not appreciating the fear of the Lord is simply the connotation of fear. The very word itself conjures up negative emotions and feelings of dread. If "fear" is a prerequisite for intimacy, how can we reconcile the two? How can we really be intimate with someone we dread? We can understand intimacy with someone we *love*— but how about someone we *fear*?

John says that perfect loves casts out fear. Fear has torment in it, but love has no fear in it (see I John 4:18 NIV). However, notice he did not say that love casts out *all* or *every* (kind) of fear. There is no contradiction between John's perfect love and the "fear of the Lord." Assuredly, those who love God perfectly will reverence Him perfectly.

John is speaking of the fear or dread that is a negative emotion. In reality it is unclean; it is sin. The fearful are leading the list of those who are headed for hell (see Revelation 21:8). On the other hand, the fear of the Lord is not a negative emotion but "...**is *clean*, enduring forever (Psalm 19:9).** Obviously there is some similarity between the *good* fear and the *bad* fear, or the Scriptures would not have employed the same word for both ideas. Whatever we may imagine those similarities are, it is very important from the outset that we recognize these fears are fundamentally different. They differ both in *nature* and in *effect*. When examining the Bible, we realize there are contradictory elements to this commodity.

When Israel stood at the bottom of Mount Sinai, it was an awesome moment. God chose that time and place to reveal Himself in very physically manifest ways. It was scary!

They did what mortal creatures should and would do. They kept their distance. Yet, God's whole purpose in manifesting Himself was to have the closest possible relationship with His people. However, their distancing themselves concerned more than just the frailty of their humanity. People can submit themselves to a fear of God that is characteristically religious.

When churches do not understand justification by faith, they easily submit to the wrong fear. When we truly cease from trying to justify ourselves, we are protected. We will be delivered from **"the spirit of bondage *again to fear"* (Romans 8:15 KJV).** Those who are still striving do not realize their condition. Though they devote themselves to much church activity with every appearance of approaching God, they do not really enjoy Him. In reality they are insecure. They cannot from the depths of their hearts become intimate. That substitute fear truly does gender bondage, preventing them from real enjoyment of God.

Unquestionably, there is a kind of religious fear of the Lord that is not the genuine. I believe a measure of that operated in the hearts of those Israelites gathered at Sinai. The genuine fear of the Lord will not torment us, or rob us of our confidence. **"In the fear of the LORD there is *strong confidence...*" (Proverbs 14:26).** Moses addresses this problem, saying to the people, **"...Do not be afraid; for God has come in order to test you, and in order that the fear of Him may remain with you, so that you may not sin" (Exodus 20:20).** In essence he says, "Do not be afraid, but do fear." God came to the people to take away one kind of fear and to replace it with another. What an exchange! Hence, though there are similarities in the two, they are fundamentally different emotions.

One of the enigmas of this commodity is how we can be happy, rejoicing people and still maintain this sober reverence for God. Christians should be characterized as people with joy indescribable and full of glory (see I Peter 1:8). Is it possible to be exuberant without being irreverent? Absolutely! David modeled it for us. With childlike abandonment he danced before the Lord. Yet, in that abandonment he did not cast off *all* restraint. He cultivated and maintained this reverential awe for the One before whom he rejoiced. Outwardly he danced and inwardly he trembled. His own expression for this is **"serve the LORD with fear and rejoice with trembling"(Psalm 2:11 KJV).** Genuine joy and fear of the Lord do not create a conflict or tension, but beautifully complement each other. **"Then you will see and be radiant, and your heart will *thrill* and *rejoice*..." (Isaiah 60:5).** What an amazing description!

There is a word translated in the Old Testament as "light" that means, "to bubble up or be frothy." This is the world's joy, and it is the best believers can do when they lose the fear of the Lord. Such joy cannot retain any semblance of sincerity. It will surely dull convictions. This characterized the pseudo-prophets with whom Jeremiah contended. God said, (they) **"cause My people to err by their lies, and by their *lightness*" (Jeremiah 23:32 KJV)**. Zephaniah 3:4 speaks of the prophets who are **"light and treacherous" (KJV)**. It is a sad day for the church when her leaders lose their inner trembling.

Finally, there is one more way we can describe the apparent enigma of this genuine fear. When Jeremiah addresses this, he puts forth an interesting question:

> **"'Am I a God who is near,' declares the LORD, 'And not a God far off?**
>
> **Can a man hide himself in hiding places, so I do not see him?' declares the LORD.**
>
> **'Do I not fill the heavens and the earth?' declares the LORD"** (Jeremiah 23:23-24).

We might suppose that when we draw near to God and He draws near to us, then He is no longer "far off." However, that is not altogether true. For Him to be near does indicate intimacy and favor (see Deuteronomy

4:7; Psalm 34:18; 69:18). **"The Lord is *near* to all who call upon Him, to all who call upon Him in truth" (Psalm 145:18).** On the other hand, He is *far* from the wicked (see Proverbs 15:29). Nevertheless, because of His majesty and greatness, there must forever remain a certain separation between God and His creatures. In this sense He must relate to us from far off. When He is far off in the sense that creatures revere Him, it will not hinder His worshipers from knowing Him in the most intimate possible way.

David describes the very familiar way that God thoroughly knows him—a way whereby David is so keenly aware of His presence. However, he describes God's knowing as occurring from afar (see Psalms 139:1-2 NIV). Jeremiah said Jehovah spoke to him in the most intimate of terms, yet this appearance occurred from afar (see Jeremiah 31:3). Therefore, if at any time He ceases to be a God "far off" simultaneously with being "near," we have lost the fear of the Lord. No matter how much we exult in our relationship, in reality God is not as near to us as we think.

Consequently, we acknowledge the gift of the office enables prophets to perceive things in the spiritual realm. Those whom God places in that ministry enjoy a relative ease of access into the heavenlies to see and hear things that are not very perceptible to some of us. However, it is a tragedy if that giftedness alone becomes the basis of receiving messages from God. God wants friends! He wants to be intimate! Such blessed communion can only happen with those who share his values and His interest. He cannot bring unrighteous people into His deliberations. Only those who truly fear Him can hope to come into His council and receive a clear word.

CHAPTER SIX

❧

THE REWARD OF DILIGENCE

To develop the thought of how we are to get *there*, we want to explore the meaning of those familiar words:

"But without faith it is impossible to please him: for he that cometh to God must believe that he is, and that he is the rewarder of them that diligently seek him (Hebrew 11:6 KJV).

These words are directed to the elect to encourage them to persevere in the faith. For the purpose of our study we specifically apply them to the process of seeking and finding God. Stated another way, we take this verse as an important promise of certainty regarding the process of encountering God.

Acts 17 records Paul's famous sermon on Mars Hill. God's purpose for placing people in their various national boundaries is summed up as follows:

"that they should seek God, if perhaps they might grope for Him and find Him, though He is not far from each one of us" (Acts 17:27).

In those words there is a wonderful description of the process of believers seeking God. However, I want to be quick to point out that God's purpose is more than a process. The end of the process is the meeting. God's purpose is that we will *find* Him through seeking. Without the finding we come short of His ultimate purpose. If we are content to go through the process without the encounter, we simply fulfill a religious duty. We are not people dedicated to reality!

The way Paul phrases the process sounds as if there are contradictory elements to the pursuit of God. He first states the process in conditional terms—he says that we are groping, with the phrase being: "if perhaps." This is not very reassuring! It really sounds like a hit-and-miss attempt to get there. Then Paul qualifies that statement with a promise that God is indeed very close to every seeker. All seekers can have the assurance that God will be found by them every time. It is guaranteed. Hence, in these two statements there is an allusion to the subjective and the objective side of the process of seeking and finding God. To illustrate this, let us go back to the very beginning when God first tested His worshipers.

After Cain slew Abel, the first parents made a new attempt to fulfill the mandate to be fruitful. Seth named their grandson Enosh. At that place in the narrative there is the brief commentary, "**…Then men began to call upon the name of the LORD" (Genesis 4:26)**. The significance of that statement might evade us if we do not recall the setting. His grandparents had known a privilege unique to humankind. Apparently it was usual fare before the Fall for the first parents to have a daily encounter with God. I surmise this from their reaction when they experienced guilt for the first time.

Their attempt to hide from God was more than an outward symptom of their effort to cover an inner feeling of culpability. They expected to meet with Elohim in a very manifest way. This was not a chance encounter, but something they anticipated at the cool of the day. I cannot verify that this happened on a daily basis. Nevertheless, judging by their response, there is no reason to think it was unusual for them to meet God regularly in this manner.

Let us elaborate on the nature of this kind of audience with God. **"And they heard the sound of the LORD God walking in the garden in the cool of the day, and the man and his wife hid themselves from the presence of the LORD God among the trees of the garden" (Genesis 3:8)**. This was more than subjectively knowing God's presence, and more than an inner awareness. In some *form* God manifested Himself to His creatures! This manifestation was fully perceptible to their physical senses. They could see Him and hear His movements through the garden. When He spoke, they heard His voice audibly. Such wonder! Now, two generations later a grandson is born who is to be the precursor of another way of meeting with God. Try to imagine the thoughts that went through the mind of that child in his youth. He could look over to the horizon in the direction of Eden and see the afterglow of God's glorious presence. He heard the stories grandfather Adam told about their experiences of visiting with God in that garden. Now the time had come for another way to be inaugurated.

This verse in Genesis is the first mention of the phrase "calling upon the name of the Lord" (see Genesis 4:26). Later on in the life of Abraham the meaning of this is modeled for us so beautifully! He who is the father of the faithful had some unusual experiences with the living God during his long lifetime. However, those unusual visitations were rare. For him the process of seeking and finding God was a real exercise of faith most of the time.

Abraham had the same battles that we have. He struggled with the same doubts, fears, feelings of apathy, and all the rest. Usually the climax of his endeavor was not an experience perceptible to his physical senses. He *found* the same way that we normally *find*. He realized the inner presence. There was that sweet peace of God settling and ordering his thoughts. There were those thoughts he could recognize as other than his own thoughts that he knew as the voice of God.

This does not mean that Adam experienced none of this. Between the Lord God's daily visit, surely there was a communion between man and God. In the original ordering of things God did not remove *all* necessity for faith. Otherwise, the first couple could not have pleased God. Without faith it is *impossible* to please Him. Nevertheless, it was undeniably different for Adam to call upon the Lord and for his progeny to do so. We are not in a protected garden. We do not have the advantage of a nature not yet plunged into depravity. We must wrestle with enemies within our souls and without. In other words, our pursuit of God necessitates a diligent activity of soul if we are going to have a meaningful experience.

The idea of pursuing God with intensity is heightened by the word the author of Hebrews chose for "seek." Hence, the King James Version of Hebrews 11:6 has added the adverb **"diligently"** to convey the intensity of our quest: **"…he is a rewarder of them that diligently seek him."** The Greek word *zeteo* in Acts 17:27 is the word often used for the meaning of "to seek," but prefixed with the preposition "after." This verse states **"that they should seek God, if perhaps they might grope for Him and find Him,**

though He is not far from each one of us." This word challenges us to literally "seek after" God. It conveys the idea that the object of our seeking is not so easy to find. It is not a casual pursuit, but a diligent search. Why must so much effort be exerted?

We mentioned the enemies both within and without that we must contend with. Besides that, our God has His own reasons for not being so accessible. Let us mention two. First, in our present mortal state we cannot experience Him in His full glory. Either He must alter His form (the way He will manifest Himself), or we must be changed. This is the limitation of our frame. A second reason concerns the exercise of faith. For God to be so accessible and freely perceptible to our physical senses would remove all necessity for faith. This accounts for many instances in the Bible where seekers came upon difficulty in finding God. **"Truly, Thou art a God who hides Himself, O God of Israel, Savior!" (Isaiah 45:15).**

Consequently, I see two extremes in which believers can align themselves in this process. There is one group who regulate their pursuit of God in an *objective* way. They are not looking for reasons or proof within themselves to know when they obtain their quest. For them the written Word of God is proof enough. The Word abounds with promises that God *will* be found by those who seek Him. Moreover, some promises state without precondition that God *is* with His people. For example, "**...I will never leave you, nor forsake you." (Hebrews 13:5** NKJV). Also, "**...for he who comes to God must believe that He is" (Hebrews 11:6** NKJV). Thus, for these brothers and sisters it is just as Paul said, "**...He is not far from each one of us" (Acts 17:27).** They do not rule out the necessity for going through the seeking process, because the Scripture commands us to do so. However, as far as they are concerned, the length of the process or the intensity of the process is not regulated by any subjective need for proof.

There are other saints whose pursuit of God is regulated by expectations that they hope to realize in a *subjective* way. Both from within and from without they are keenly sensitive to hindrances they feel with respect to the enjoyment of His presence. They expect God to reward their pursuit with some kind of breakthrough, causing a subjective realization of His presence. Until they realize this climax, they are not satisfied that they have obtained the reward that our text promises.

Consequently, their times of pursuit may have some irregularity. Who can say what all the factors are that make a difference from one day to the next? What regulates whether God is near or far? Why do enemy spirits resist us more on one day than another? Hence, these variables make the pursuit of God like one who is groping into the unseen. Some days the battles seem fiercer. On days like that they must stay longer to prevail. They must persevere in their seeking until they know they have obtained that which they seek.

Obviously, there are strengths and weaknesses in both modes of seeking. I conclude that every believer's pursuit of God needs to include both the objective and subjective aspect. To the credit of those who regulate their prayers only by what they see in the written Word, there is stability in their devotion. Also, there is usually regularity. What they *feel* simply does not enter into the process. On the other hand, the weakness of their approach lies in finding satisfaction too easily. They may conclude their prayer, when the Lord is seeking to draw them into a deeper experience. What about those who are too far on the subjective side?

If they limit their satisfaction only to what they can realize subjectively, they expose themselves too much to the enemy. Our feelings are very vulnerable! In fact, there comes a point in this kind of seeking when it ceases to be faith at all. To persist in it can become a statement of unbelief. I think this is especially true for churches that emphasize experiences. Expecting too much subjective fulfillment is problem enough; there is something else that complicates their pursuit of God.

If those churches do not have a sound doctrinal basis for justification by faith, the situation really becomes complex! Their prayer life becomes legalistic and a religious duty. Seeking God becomes a subtle attempt to gain acceptance with Him. Regardless of the pitfalls, we commend this group for their sensitiveness to be led beyond their present level of experience. They allow their expectations to be gratified only by a live encounter with God.

With these preliminary remarks concerning two modes of seeking, let us raise some questions. We began this chapter with the promise that God rewards diligence. How can those who pray know when they have obtained that reward? If we have had a season of prayer and reach an inner satisfaction through that exertion of soul, is that enough? If the perceived obstacles that were there in the beginning of this pursuit have receded into the background and the peace of God rules in our heart, have we persisted far enough? If there is an inner calm accompanied by a sense of God speaking, is that sufficient? Generally speaking, we can answer affirmatively. Nevertheless, what sincere seeker has not wondered at times if there would be a greater breakthrough, if he would just give himself more to the process?

If we *are* inclined to pursue more diligently, is it out of order for us to be specific about our expectations? If we realize that the objective modes of transition are advantageous, can we desire this? Listen to the psalmist:

"As the deer pants for the water brooks, so my soul pants for Thee, O God. My soul thirsts for God, for the living God; When shall I come and appear before God?" (Psalm 42:1-2)

What exactly was this person expecting? What would perfectly satisfy those aspirations? In the following verses he recalls former times when he participated in the religious festivals of Israel. Is he expressing restlessness, waiting for the next festival, or is he saying that even festivals do not satisfy his longings? Regardless of whether festivals satisfied him or not, we still need a clearer idea concerning his expectations.

One of the privileges of the Old Testament people was to have the glory (see Romans 9:4). What happened at Sinai was not the last time God manifested Himself to His people in ways that are perceptible to the physical senses. The Shekinah glory was their common privilege! When David expresses his desire to be in God's temple and **"behold the beauty of the LORD" (Psalm 27:4)**, he is not using a figure of speech. If he only anticipated a subjective experience whereby God would be real in his heart, he could have that in his times of communion out in the pasture.

He did not need to be in the temple. He could realize his desires under more normal circumstances. He evidently alludes to something richer than the normal subjective climaxes the believer has when seeking God.

In the New American Standard version of the preceding quotation, the expression concerning appearing before God is weaker than some other translations. Young's renders it, **"When do I enter and see the face of God?"** The Revised Standard Version and Lamsa's translation are about the same. We can only speculate as to precisely what the psalmist expected as an answer to his seeking. Had he been living in the New Testament era, we might associate it with the words of Paul.

Paul said that when we are absent from the body, we are present with the Lord. He spoke of being with the Lord as the ultimate satisfaction. Of course, in those passages he refers to the transition in death. I doubt that death is what those saints anticipated. The eternal state was not so clear to the Old Testament community. They did not have expectations as we do for our heavenly home. They aspired to experience the goodness of the Lord in the land of the living. Consequently, for God to come and reveal Himself in a more manifest way *here* and *now* was certainly at the heart of the psalmist's yearnings.

In conclusion, we say with the psalmist,

"How blessed is the one whom Thou dost choose, and bring near to Thee, to dwell in Thy courts. We will be satisfied with the goodness of Thy house, Thy holy temple" (Psalm 65:4).

The aspirant in the psalm uses the Old Testament imagery of the temple and the courts to describe nearness to God. However, as we illustrated above with David, those aspirations go beyond the natural and yearn for the spiritual.

In this study we have laid out a proximity to God in terms that go beyond our normal subjective encounter. We have boldly broached the possibility of these phenomenal experiences becoming the reward for our diligence. To what extent God in His sovereignty chooses some to stand in His presence in these unusual ways, and to what extent the invitation is left open to whosoever will, is open to speculation. The Scripture gives no clear rule. Nevertheless, some things are surely promised to all who draw near to God in faith. We can be certain that He rewards diligent seeking. We also know that this reward contains within it the satisfaction of which the psalmist speaks.

CHAPTER SEVEN

❧❦❧

THE DELIBERATIONS
OF GOD

All through our study we have spoken matter-of-factly about God deliberating in a council. Such an idea certainly evokes many questions. Does a sovereign God *really* counsel with *any* of His creatures? Does the word a prophet receives from heaven have its origins in a conclave where it is deliberated? If that word was deliberated, does that allow for contingencies in its fulfillment? We could add other questions, but this will suffice to lay the groundwork for this chapter. Let us begin with a look at the sovereignty of God.

In some statements, Paul makes no allowance for the idea of a deliberating sovereign. He says that He made known to us the mystery of His will, "**...according to his good pleasure which he hath purposed in himself...being predestined according to the purpose of him who worketh all things after the counsel of his own will.**" **(Ephesians 1:9,11** KJV). Isaiah asks the probing question, "**Who has directed the**

Spirit of the LORD, or as His counselor has informed Him? With whom did He consult and who gave Him understanding? And who taught Him in the path of justice and taught Him knowledge, and informed Him of the way of understanding?"(Isaiah 40:13-14).

The inference of these questions is clear. There is *no one* who answers to those roles! There are so many verses that portray Him as sovereign in the true sense of the word. Portions that portray Him differently must be reconciled with His majesty. We must understand passages that depict Him as deliberating only as expressions of how He condescends to interact with His creatures. Thus, it remains for us now to try to comprehend the sense in which He has chosen to do this.

The scenes of the throne room in Revelation supply us with more information than any other portion of Scripture. Supposing that the twenty-four elders depict a heavenly council, their response to each situation agrees with what we would expect God's *sode* to be like. God discusses nothing. In each scenario He Who sits on the throne has decreed things while the rest agree. They express their hearty consent with "Amen's" and acts of worship. In each scene angelic creatures and redeemed human beings are adoring spectators, not advisors. However, one incident may shed light on our subject.

One of the angels raised the question, "...**Who is worthy to open the book and to break its seals?**"**(Revelation 5:2)** It seems God granted them opportunity to search for one who answered to those qualifications. For a while no one was found! This may seem like a game, but God does not play games with His creatures. There is nothing insincere about God ordering events this way. It only illustrates His willingness to condescend and His desire to interact with us. He is so personal! What great yearnings for fellowship reside within His heart! I cannot say how long that search transpired or how they conducted it, but it was no game to John. He cried until someone reassured him there is someone in heaven who qualifies.

There is another lesson in this scene. When John considered the possibility that a qualified one may not exist, he might have consoled himself with thoughts concerning the sovereignty of God. He could have said, "I do not understand this, but I know God has everything under control. I will just quietly wait and see." That line of reasoning would certainly be true. Sometimes the tests of faith are so great, it is the *only* line of reasoning we can take. Nevertheless, John could not respond so simply as that. Contingencies were very real to him!

You would think that if there were any place in the entire universe where a creature could have those reassuring thoughts, it would be in the throne room. Everything there speaks of the fact that there is, and always will be One upon the throne who serenely reigns above all the difficulties of life. There is One who always has everything under control. Yet, in that setting it was possible for John to feel that there are contingencies. Even in heaven He still could privately entertain his doubts. Therefore, let us not suppose that audience in the throne room precludes the possibility of us seeing and responding to things in a very human way. Furthermore, there is a sense in which events around the throne do not transpire in a deterministic way. From John's perspective, there were contingencies.

There are other throne room scenes that have bearing upon our subject. When Isaiah had his divine appointment, he first had to confront his own uncleanness. After he felt the burning coal from the altar of God's holiness, he then heard the voice of the Lord saying, **"Whom shall I send, and who will go for Us?" (Isaiah 6:8)** What an amazing scene this is!

This is not an angel speaking to other angels. God is speaking. He does not express His will as a proclamation, but as something He deliberates! The subject is first "I" and then becomes "us." It would be convenient to claim this as simple proof of plurality of persons in the Godhead. In other words, the "us" could represent the members of the Trinity and not the council. This would mean that the Godhead is deliberating and the council is consenting like the elders in Revelation.

Even if that were the case, it still portrays God as expressing His will in a deliberative fashion. There is no indication from this scene that other members of the court expressed anything, but they were certainly attentive. A question implies that an answer is expected, and an answer there was! Isaiah spoke up, in essence volunteering himself. God accepted his offer, commissioning him with a message for the people. If there is a clear example of one who stood in the council of God and came forth from that place with a commission and a message, we have one here.

I am not saying that in every case it requires a sensational experience like this in order to qualify a person as one who has stood in the council of the Lord. However, I do say this is unquestionably a case of that happening. Furthermore, I contend that we should not relegate these experiences to another era, but allow it to happen today. God still gives free access to His servants to be in the midst of those who are standing by.

Returning to the thought of contingencies, we may assume that this was a divine setup. In other words, Isaiah had that audience only because he was going to be commissioned.

Amos 3:7 states, **"Surely the Lord GOD does nothing unless He reveals His *secret counsel* to His servants the prophets."** That does not necessarily mean He is revealing it with the sole purpose of commissioning them to speak.

If the Almighty is condescending and so desirous of having angels around Him when He is deliberating, is it strange that He should desire to bring some of His redeemed children into this fellowship? It would be a mistake to reason that the only purpose for standing in the council of God is so they can run with a message. God really does desire fellowship. On the other hand, if people *do* claim to have a commission, we have a right to look for evidence that they indeed stood in that place.

Our final scene is found in the message of Micaiah to Ahab where he says,

> **"I saw the LORD sitting on His throne, and all the host of heaven standing by Him on His right hand and on His left.**
>
> **And the LORD said, 'Who will entice Ahab to go up and fall at Ramoth-Gilead?' And one said this while another said that.**
>
> **Then a spirit came forward and stood before the Lord and said, 'I will entice him.'**

**And the LORD said to him, 'How?'
And he said, 'I will go out and be a
deceiving spirit in the mouth of all
his prophets.' Then He said, 'You
are to entice him and also prevail.
Go and do so.'"** (I Kings 22:19-22).

This scene gives more latitude for our
present discussion than the two we have
already discussed. First, recalling Isaiah's
experience, we now see the roles reversed.
Here the prophet silently observes, while the
angels respond to the questions. Moreover,
now it is not a simple one-question, one-
answer scenario. Rather, **"one said this
while another said that."** This is amazing!
Can there really be that much deliberation
in the council room of heaven? Apparently
there is.

However, we must say again that scenes
like this are displaying the side of the coin
that reveals God's condescension to fellowship
with His creatures. The other side of the coin
reveals His sovereignty. To illustrate, once
the Lord Jesus asked a disciple, "Where are
we to buy bread, that these may eat?" John's
record says it succinctly: (The Lord) **"Himself
knew what He was intending to do" (John
6:6).** That statement says it all! The Lord
Jesus asked the disciples, yet He knew what
He intended to do. We must keep both sides
of the coin before us lest we end up with a
distorted view of God.

Taking our thoughts a step further, could there be a case of an Isaiah who has been granted audience and volunteers, when in reality it is not the Father's perfect will? In other words, are there those whom God brings into His intimacy, but not for the purpose of sending them on an errand? If this is possible, I believe it accounts for some of the inaccuracies that occur today in prophetic ministry. I anticipate when the Lord *does* accept the offer of an Isaiah, it *will* be His perfect will. It will be His timing, His vessel, and the message will be clear. Or, if it is the case of a "Micaiah" silently observing, could he not withdraw himself prematurely from that place and fail to have the final words of those deliberations? In that case the prophet would only have part of the message. These questions may sound like vain speculation, but I think they follow logically from the analogy of the throne scenes.

To conclude, many have criticized prophetic ministry today. There is not much tolerance for prophecies that failed to come true. Some have risen to the defense of the prophets, trying to show that there are conditions necessary for the fulfillment. One credible national brother boldly states that *all* prophecy, whether clearly stated or not is conditional. He does qualify this fact by saying there is a level of prophecy—something on the order of God making a covenant—that is sheer proclamation of God's intentions. He says in that case what God declares will surely happen.

At any rate, no matter how men try to explain it, the fact remains that prophetic words today do not compare with their counterpart in the Old Testament. The majority of the examples we have in the Old Testament are messengers who came forth from the presence of the Lord, declared how things will be, and it happened that way. It is not unreasonable for saints today to desire to see it again like it was then. On the one hand, my aim in doing a study like this *is* to step forward with a defense for the prophets. Consequently, I seek to hold forth a higher standard for accuracy in prophetic words.

A final illustration will suffice. The Bible records Jonah's message to the Ninevites. **"...Yet forty days and Nineveh will be overthrown!" (Jonah 3:4)** We all know the outcome of the event. Jonah was wrong! It did not happen in forty days! The Bible verifies Jonah's credentials. Jehovah sent him with a *mission* and a *message*. The Son of God Himself takes liberty to cite Jonah's experience as an important prophetic sign to future generations. There is no mistake about it—Jonah was a servant of the Lord. He was not a false prophet in the true meaning, even though his prophecy did not come to pass.

If we accept that Jonah was truly sent by God, we then have a dilemma concerning God's ways. Did God not know beforehand that the Ninevites would repent? Is there vacillation in His will? I will let the theologian A.W. Pink answer this for us:

"In order to understand certain passages it is absolutely needful to recognize that there is a *twofold* "will" of God spoken of in the Scriptures, by which we do not mean His decretive will and His permissive will, for in the final analysis that is a distinction without a difference, for God never permits anything that is contrary to His eternal purpose. No, we refer to the very real distinction that there is between His *secret* and His *revealed* will, or, as we much prefer to express it, between His *predestinated* and His *preceptive* will. God's secret will is His own counsels that He has divulged to no one. His revealed will is made known in His Word, and is the definer of our duty and the standard of our responsibility. The grand reason why I should follow a certain course or do a certain thing is because it is God's will that I should do so—made known to me in the rule I am to walk by. But suppose I go contrary to His Word and disobey, have I not crossed His will? Assuredly. Then does that mean that I have thwarted His purpose? Certainly not, for that is always accomplished, notwithstanding the perversity of His creatures. God's revealed will is never performed perfectly by any of us, but His secret or foreordinating will is never prevented by any" (see Psalms 135:6; Proverbs 21:30; Isaiah.46:10).

Certainly God *did* know the Ninevites would repent. Therefore, one explanation is that God did not divulge the outcome simply because it was part of His secret will. He has His reasons. A second possibility is that Jonah only heard part of the message. It would be like the proposition we raised above concerning the scenario Micaiah described. In other words, Jonah left God's council before hearing all the deliberations. A third possibility is that he heard it all, but his prejudices prevented him from giving a complete proclamation. Perhaps the complete message of the deliberations of the heavenly council was: **"...Yet forty days and Nineveh will be overthrown" (Jonah 3:4),** *unless she repents.*

When God sent Jonah to go to Ninevah the first time, it does not tell us there is a specific message. His commission was merely to go, and cry out against the sins of the city. That was his *mission*. That was the central purpose of the Lord. The second time after being re-commissioned, the Lord tells him to go and He will tell him what to say. We assume that Jonah said what the Lord told him to say, if not in whole, at least in part. Consequently, though the message was not accomplished, the mission was.

God's people should rejoice when the mission is accomplished, but Jonah was greatly upset over this discrepancy. He vented his displeasure toward the Lord. God in turn mildly reproved him for not rejoicing that the mission was accomplished *even though the word was not*. The church today is too smart to become upset with the Lord in contemporary situations like the Jonah-Nineveh scenario. Consequently, when words do not happen, we vent our displeasure toward His "Jonah's." Nevertheless, are we any different from Jonah if we fail to rejoice in accomplished missions even if it means that the accomplishment will sometimes contradict the message of the messenger?

I want to say again that I am not promoting looseness or carelessness in prophetic ministry. There needs to be greater accuracy and maturing in the use of prophetic gifts. For the one example we have like Jonah, we have many others that turned out differently. The prophets spoke of coming judgments and it happened. In some prophetic strains the message is strict, making no allowance for even repentance to turn it back. The evil had progressed too far too long. They are quite different in Nineveh's case. Hence, we regard those stricter situations as unalterable ultimatums from the throne. Those examples agree with what most of us expect prophecy to be like. Obviously all prophecy is not like that so we must give latitude for each case.

Therefore, if we evaluate prophets today in terms of Isaiah's question, we should understand the standard. We need to understand better the dynamics and transactions of God's council. We must understand the meaning of His messengers standing there. There certainly is a level of prophecy that is an unalterable ultimatum. There are no contingencies regulating the fulfillment. There are no more deliberations, unless to determine which spirit will go forth, or which Isaiah will be the messenger. On the other hand, there is also prophecy as in the case of Jonah. Regardless of whether the messengers know it, or whether they declare it, there are conditions with the message.

Consequently, if the Lord's "Jonah's" today are not prejudiced, but sincerely seeking to be a clear channel of communication, we should look for other reasons for prophetic declarations not happening. Probably the way they stand in the council of the Lord is the cause for inaccurate words. I expect the discrepancy concerns an inability to distinguish the difference between God's *ultimatums* (which are unconditional), and His *proclamations* (which allow for contingencies).

CHAPTER EIGHT

❦

PARAMETERS

Bringing loose ends together from various things we discussed, let us make some applications. I will summarize with four points. We have said much by way of example from both the Old Testament and New Testament period to establish a biblical norm for describing the experiences of prophetic ministry. I have endeavored to expose prejudices of our Western mind-set. I have confronted preconceived notions concerning acceptable modes for communicating with God. I discussed things that many of us are personally unfamiliar—things that make us uncomfortable. Nevertheless, it is not right for us to hold up our own experience, or even the experience of the majority of God's people as a standard for the church today. If these remarkable mystical experiences were part of the ministry of people of the Bible, we must make allowance for them in the church today. Therefore, my first admonition is let us not treat the mystical experiences of the Lord's ministers as something weird.

When Peter went to Jerusalem to give an account of his new directive from heaven, those elders had the burden to judge what that message was. Trying to decide if the centurion *really* saw an angel of God did not distract them. They might easily have reasoned that since he was a Gentile (unbeliever), then he could only get it from the wrong source. Surely it was an experience of the occult, they might have surmised. If we had been with those elders seated before Ezekiel when he was on his trip, how would we respond to his subliminal state? Was he kneeling in our favorite posture for prayer or was he positioned like those in Eastern religions during their times of meditation? We are too concerned today with *how* visionaries get their revelations, rather than with *what* the revelation is!

If standing in the council of the Lord involves having free access among cherubim, seraphim, or any other angelic creatures standing by, we must make allowance for this in our understanding of the matter. In the letter to the Colossians, Paul discusses the problem of a wrong kind of mysticism. However, he does not (as some might suppose) condemn out of hand those who see angels. Just the matter of seeing angels is not treated as a taboo. The Old Testament saints and the early church treated visions beyond the veil rather matter-of-factly. Consequently, if we do not also treat it that way, an ambiance of suspicion will pervade the church. It will be difficult for prophets to offer themselves to the Holy Spirit for whatever mode He deems best to communicate with them.

My next admonition is: May we not have an unwholesome fascination with visions beyond the veil. This may sound like a contradiction to the above, but it is not. We should treat these mystical experiences as acceptable, but keep the right perspective. Recall for a moment the difference in the response of Samson's mother and his father after the angel appeared to them, telling them how to raise the boy (see Judges 13:1-23). The mother, who was calm and matter-of-fact, was intent on what the message of the Lord was. By contrast, the father was excited and somewhat fearful. He felt he had to know the name of the messenger. This inquiry was not an exercise in discernment. In other words, he did not question that the angel was from God. He just felt he had to know the angel's name. If we are going to be excessively fascinated, it would be better that fearful describe the way we feel rather than sensational. Hype and sensationalism are too much a part of the American church scene. The demeanor of Samson's mother is a good example for those relating their spiritual experiences.

When Paul describes those who are mystical in the wrong way, he says, "**...the**

worship of the angels, taking his stand on visions he has seen, inflated without cause by his fleshly mind, and not holding fast to the Head..." (Colossians 2:18-19). In John's vision when he was caught up into heaven, toward the end he is tempted to fall down before his angelic guide. How does heaven respond to this misdirected affection? Is he sternly rebuked and warned to stay away from angels? On the contrary! The angel mildly corrects him, telling him to worship God only (see Revelation 19:10). This is another amazing example of how a believer can be caught away in the Spirit to the very throne room of God and still be so human, even to the point of possibly erring! Consider the implications of this.

If this John was an apostle, and I believe that he was, he was not a novice to the faith. He was very elderly, a seasoned saint. In Revelation 1, he experienced the glory of the risen Christ. He also saw the majesty of Him who sits upon the throne. He observed all heaven directing their worship to Him. Now, at the end of all that experience and convincing evidence, he is tempted to let his affections go out more than it should toward an angel.

If this seasoned man of God can be tempted like that, I do not entertain much hope that we are going to be more discrete. Surely we will be unnecessarily fascinated sometimes, and we will be carried away for a season. It is to be hoped that we will quickly learn and regain our equilibrium. At any rate we should be realistic about this issue. The solution is not to shun all mystical experiences. Moreover, let us realize that what I just described does not really correspond to the error Paul addresses in the book of Colossians.

Those Colossian mystics were not carried away only occasionally in their fascination with angels. They were intentionally and habitually directing their attention there. They were vain. Whether they actually saw angels (maybe even conversing with them), or were deceived in their imagination—it is not clear from the text. Regardless, their emphasis was in the wrong place. They were not centered on Christ, nor did they appreciate His church. They esteemed their own spiritual experiences above the written Word of God. In a word, they were aloof from the rest of the church.

We have all met these super-spiritual ones that Paul describes, but is that really what we are dealing with today in the prophetic controversy? Is that not different from sincere believers who truly love the Lord Jesus, give finality to the written Word, and esteem their place in the body of Christ, but become too enamored with spiritual experiences? Adjustment is in order, but stopping mystical experiences is not.

Consider Paul's brief commentary of his trip to the third heaven. He said he heard unutterable sayings that He was not permitted to speak. Does that mean he feels restrained to be as brief as possible about the details, or that he should not talk at all about what he saw and heard? Was this a restraint the Holy Spirit placed upon him only, or is he a model for us all? If he is saying categorically that those scenes and experiences behind the veil are to remain veiled, we are left with an enigma. Why did God commission John, Isaiah, Ezekiel, and others to talk about their experiences *in great detail*? What is the significance of Paul's statement? **"...which a man is not permitted to speak" (II Corinthians 12:4).**

Please notice he did not say that he is not permitted to tell his experience, nor even to talk about what he saw. God restrained him from repeating something that he particularly heard on that visit. John, likewise, had a similar experience. He described many things he saw and heard, but was forbidden to tell what the seven peals of thunder uttered (see Revelation 10:4). Paul and John are cases of special restrictions, but not examples of the way all men of the Bible handled their experiences. Nevertheless, given our penchant for the flare and the sensational, we should take the stricter interpretation, emulating Paul's cautious demeanor.

A third admonition is: May we all be challenged to greater diligence in seeking and finding God. If some in our midst are having unusual transitions beyond the veil, that should not intimidate us, or leave us with a complex that we are second-class citizens. Rather, it should stir our own desires and expectations. The promises of God are sure, but not so specific. He is rich unto *all* who call upon Him. He does reward diligence. It remains to be seen how rich and how rewarding that can be. I have tried to make a case for the church recognizing these exceptional transitions as the privilege of the prophetic office. At the same time, I have also extended it to whosoever will. It is incumbent upon those who *do* have the privilege of the office to use it humbly. Those who are experiencing ways to walk among those who are standing by must guard their hearts against feelings of elitism. For the rest of us, let God's favor to them challenge us to greater diligence.

Granted that more of us can have extraordinary encounters, we need guidelines to regulate intense pursuit. I said that there is an objective and a subjective aspect to seeking and finding. I submit that if our prayer life is rather routine then we are too objective. We need to hear the call of the Spirit to deeper communion. That may require us to give more time to the process. If our hearts are guarded against elitism and self-righteousness, and we are purely motivated like the psalmist to see the face of God, who can fault us for this? If we can sustain a more intense pursuit without getting out of rest, or without loosing the peace of God that surpasses understanding, our endeavor is on course. If our hearts are persuaded that the basis of our acceptance is Christ and not our works, we are proceeding from the right foundation. However, if our pursuit gets us out of rest, we need to move back to a more objective position and reassess the matter.

Finally, we should make allowance for emerging prophets to mature in their ministry. We have raised many questions about the nature of God's *sode*. The idea of deliberation at the throne may be new to some of us, but I trust I have treated the Scriptures faithfully. There *are* contingencies in prophecy. There *are* justifiable reasons why true prophets of God proclaim a word that does not happen. Nonetheless, we have held forth a higher standard for accuracy than we presently see today.

I think it is foolish for anyone to speculate or even suggest what the level of accuracy should presently be. It makes a great difference in the kind of prophecies we are considering. If we are talking about the "run-of-the mill" themes such as, "The Lord is coming soon," or "I love you," says the Lord, how can we be inaccurate? On the other hand, if we are talking about predicting events, (being specific with names, places, and even dates) where are those who do this with a consistently high level of accuracy?

If we will be honest with the real issue concerning those pseudo-prophets God rebukes through his servant Jeremiah, the problem is not what we might suppose. The problem there concerned their failure to turn Israel away from sin. Accuracy in foretelling the future was expected. It was a basic condition for the Old Testament office. However, it was not the central issue of Jehovah's rebuke.

The issue was sin in the life of the prophets. The offense concerned their using their ministry to strengthen the evil lifestyle of Israel. Stated another way, the question of whether individuals had stood in the council of God hinged on whether their message was leading the people to greater holiness or to greater compromise:

> **"But if they had stood in My council, then they would have announced My words to My people, and would have turned them back from their evil way and from the evil of their deeds"** **(Jeremiah 23:22).**

There are individuals among us today emerging in the prophetic office who have a heart for the Lord. They hold forth for themselves and the audiences they address commendable standards. Some of them have sincerely tried to move out of the status quo. They have gone out on a limb to predict future events. In doing so, they have some-times missed. Unfortunately, the church has not been too tolerant of this. I think it unfair that we would cast them into the same mold with the false prophets of the Old Testament. It is not right to say that they totally failed to stand in the council of the Lord. When the main thrust of their preaching is to promote holiness in the church, we should cut them some slack in their prophesying. Having said that, this opens up a scary prospect.

The church suffers for lack of experience and maturity in the prophetic office. There is a desire to see greater accuracy. We want the true ones to hone their skills. However, if that means giving them license to practice by publicly pointing out people's sins, that is unsettling. I am not making a case for salving our conscience, saying it is out of character for God to ever do things that way. Let us not deceive ourselves. God is still in the business of exposing hidden sins. Neverthe-less, when emerging prophets attempt to be God's channel for this and are inaccurate, the damage is great. Even in the more impressive cases when the revelation is accurate but not used with wisdom, the church still suffers.

The church cannot bear this kind of training and practice. So, whereas I appeal for greater tolerance for emerging prophets who may miss on their predictions of events, I do not make a case for their being reckless with people's lives.

Finally, let us recall the way Paul showed the Corinthians to cultivate manifestations of the Spirit in their midst. I Corinthians 13, the famous love chapter is often taught to expound the virtues of *agape*. However, when some expositors get through treating that chapter, they end up with a divergent conclusion. They say if we have love, we no longer need the manifestations of the Spirit. Truly, Paul says that love is eternal and the manifestations are not. There is some truth in saying that love replaces the gifts, but it misses the thrust of why Paul brings it up in the first place. For expositors to make that conclusion, they must lift I Corinthians 13 out of the context of the preceding chapter and the one that follows.

In the context of those two chapters he does not expound love as a thing or a commodity. In other places in Scripture, love is described that way. For example, in Galatians, love is one of the fruits of the Spirit. Fruit is one thing and gifts are another. We must not compare their characteristics and purpose so as to make them mutually exclusive of one another. So, whereas there is a sense that love is a thing, Paul expounds it to the Corinthians as a way.

It is the more excellent way for gifts of the Spirit to happen. Faith is the most basic way, hope is a more mature way, and love is the greatest of the three. Consequently, believers who only operate in faith will have keenness about them. They will see the value of these gifts and earnestly desire them. That is certainly a climate for spiritual manifestations to happen. Yet, such an environment might lend itself to competition. In our zeal to function we may lack thoughtfulness for the other person who wishes also to be used by the Spirit. However, if the climate is love, we will not be afraid of making mistakes. There is a greater encouragement for us to use our gifts and thereby grow in experience.

Consequently, we should aspire to have the environment of *love* in our churches. Love is the excellent way. It is the best way for the Spirit to manifest Himself through the parts of the body. It is the ideal situation for brothers and sisters to learn to use their gifts. It is the best environment to train those who are developing in ministry. May those who are emerging today in the prophetic office not have to struggle through a hostile climate, but find the encouragement of a church that is characterized by love.

To summarize these four points, first let us face up to our prejudices and return to a biblical position concerning mystical experiences. We must not treat them as weird. Next, having restored these experiences to their rightful place, let us keep our equilibrium. They are merely a means to an end, not something to become too fascinated with. Third, may all of God's people be challenged to a more diligent pursuit of God. These experiences are a legitimate part of the prophetic office, but the Lord wants to grant richer encounters to *all* who seek Him. Finally, let us provide a friendly climate for emerging prophets to mature in their office. Now abides faith, hope, love, these three; the greatest of these is love (see I Corinthians 13:13). Love is the greatest way for gifts to happen and for ministry to mature. If the church will cultivate a loving environment, in a few years she will receive a prophet's reward. May God grant it to be so!